QuickBooks Online

For Beginners

The Step By Step Guide for Small Business
Owners. How to Master QuickBooks and
Speed up Bookkeeping without Stress

Rob Harris

Table of contents

Introduction

You have arrived to the correct location if you are the proprietor of a small company and are interested in streamlining the bookkeeping and accounting procedures at your company. QuickBooks Online is an extremely powerful tool that may assist you in managing your finances, keeping track of your revenue and spending, and generating reports that can assist you in making educated business choices. If you are interested in learning more about QuickBooks Online, read here.

This all-encompassing book will teach you everything you need to know about QuickBooks Online, from setting up an account to entering transactions to running reports and beyond. You will learn how to get the most out of QuickBooks Online by taking use of all of its features, such as the ability to handle inventory and invoices, as well as payroll and other employee benefits.

But before we get into the specifics, let's first discuss what QuickBooks Online is and why it is such a helpful tool for business owners to have at their disposal.

You can manage your money at any time and from any location with the help of QuickBooks Online, which is accounting software that is hosted in the cloud. It offers a variety of tools that may increase productivity, simplify operations, and give insight into strategic decision-making, and it was developed with the requirements of small firms in mind. Whether you run a one-person operation or employ a huge team of people, QuickBooks Online is a helpful tool that can help you manage the finances of your company and remain on top of the cash flow in your business.

One of the most notable advantages of QuickBooks Online is its intuitive user interface. There is no need for accounting experience or previous acquaintance with the program, and neither of those things is required. Because both the interface and the functionality of QuickBooks Online are so uncomplicated, the software is very easy to learn and use.

In spite of this, QuickBooks Online is a powerful accounting tool in addition to its user-friendliness, making it a particularly attractive option. You'll be able to better manage the financial aspects of your company with the assistance of the automatic bank feeds, invoicing, and expenditure monitoring tools offered by QuickBooks Online. Additionally, due to the fact that it is web-based, you are able to log in to your account anytime you choose from any device that is linked to the internet.

It should come as no surprise that the security of any web-based application is a primary concern. Because the protection and safety of your financial information is of the utmost importance, QuickBooks Online makes use of a number of different precautions. When you use QuickBooks Online, the safety of the information you keep about your finances is guaranteed.

This tutorial will lead you through everything, from registering for an account to customizing QuickBooks Online to meet the requirements of your company, step by step. We are going to explore the different functions that are available in QuickBooks Online and show you how to put them to use so that you may better manage your finances. By the time you've finished reading this book, you'll have a thorough understanding of QuickBooks Online and be able to use it to your advantage, whether that means reducing the amount of time you spend on administrative tasks, boosting your productivity at work, or making more well-informed choices.

So, let's get started!

Chapter 1

Why QuickBooks Online is Safe to Use

In the modern day, protecting sensitive customer information is a primary concern for companies of all kinds. Companies have a responsibility to take precautions in order to safeguard their sensitive financial data in light of the growing risk posed by cyberattacks and data breaches. When it comes to accounting software, QuickBooks Online is a well-liked option for small companies owing to the fact that it is convenient, inexpensive, and adaptable. However, it is only normal to be concerned about the safety of your financial data if you use any cloud-based program.

In this chapter, we will discuss the safety features and precautions that are taken by QuickBooks Online in order to protect the information you keep about your financial transactions. To get things started, let's talk about what QuickBooks Online is and how it differs from more conventional accounting software. After that, we'll get into why having software that you can trust is so important for businesses and why data security is so important for companies in general. In this section, we will discuss the many security features that are available via QuickBooks Online. Some of these features include data encryption, secure login methods, and access restrictions. In addition, we will talk about integrations with third-party services and how QuickBooks Online protects the safety of these connections.

You will have a solid knowledge of why QuickBooks Online is a safe and secure solution for small companies by the time you reach the conclusion of this chapter. These firms are trying to simplify their accounting procedures.

What is QuickBooks Online?

QuickBooks Online is accounting software that is hosted in the cloud and is aimed to assist small companies in more effectively managing their financial affairs. It provides customers with a range of tools that make it possible for them to produce and send invoices, manage spending, reconcile bank transactions, generate financial reports, and more. Because it can be accessed from any location as long as there is an internet connection, QuickBooks Online is a practical choice for companies that need to operate away from the office or while traveling.

monticello/Depositphotos.com

One of the most important advantages provided by QuickBooks Online is the fact that it is a program that operates on the cloud. This is among the most essential advantages. This signifies that all of your financial information is kept on secure servers, and that these servers are accessible from any device so long as it has an internet connection. Moreover, these servers are safeguarded from unauthorized access by many layers of security. This eliminates the need for businesses to keep data on their own computers, which might expose the data to potential security concerns such as theft, fire, or the failure of the underlying technology. Instead, organizations can store data on a third-party server. If a company uses software that is hosted in the cloud, it may be possible for them to save both time and money when it comes to the expense of maintaining and upgrading their software.

In addition, there are a number of significant distinctions between conventional accounting software and QuickBooks Online, which is an online version of the desktop program. For example, typical accounting software is generally installed on a single computer and can only be accessed from that computer. This restriction prevents the program from being shared across other computers. It is not possible for users to access the program via any other device. It's possible that this might be a limiting issue for businesses who require access to their financial data from a variety of places or devices.

Traditional accounting software may be time-consuming and tedious to both set up and understand, in addition to being costly to both purchase and keep up to date.

On the other hand, QuickBooks Online was designed to be user-friendly and its installation procedure was made to be as easy as possible. It provides a variety of pricing options to cater to businesses of varying sizes and requirements, ranging from a basic plan that is suitable for sole proprietors and freelancers to more comprehensive plans that are better suited for larger companies that have more intricate accounting requirements. These pricing options can be found on the company's website.

QuickBooks Online includes a variety of interfaces with third-party apps and services, such as those for payroll and payment processing, in order to aid companies in the process of simplifying their financial operations. This is one of the primary goals of QuickBooks Online. When data is input manually into many systems, it may be a time-consuming process that also comes with a high risk of making errors. This might assist save time and reduce the likelihood of such dangers occurring.

The Importance of Data Security

Intuit, the firm that provides QuickBooks Online, is in charge of maintaining the safety of all of the servers that keep your company's financial information when you use the cloud-based software QuickBooks Online. While this does have a number of advantages, such as remote access and automated backups, it also means that your data is susceptible to security risks, such as hacking, data breaches, and cyber-attacks. While this does have a number of advantages, such as remote access and automatic backups, it also means that your data is vulnerable. As a result, it is essential to take the necessary precautions to safeguard your data and guarantee that it cannot be accessed by unauthorized parties.

Here are some of the key reasons why data security is important when using QuickBooks Online:

Protects sensitive financial information

Your company's sensitive financial data is among the most important and confidential information that it owns. It contains information about your revenue, spending, invoices, and bank accounts, in addition to facts about your customers and staff that are personally identifiable. If this information is obtained by unauthorized parties, it opens the door to identity theft, fraud, and other types of financial crimes. As a result, it is very necessary to maintain the confidentiality of this information.

Maintains customer trust

If the information of your customers, such as credit card data, is handled by your company, it is imperative that this information be protected so that your consumers will continue to have faith in your company. Customers have an expectation that the information they provide will be kept private and safe; if you fail to meet this expectation, it may be detrimental to your reputation and result in a loss of business.

Compliance with regulations

It is possible that you are needed to comply with specific data security standards, such as the General Data Protection Regulation (GDPR) or the Health Insurance Portability and Accountability Act (HIPAA), but this will depend on the industry that you work in. Should you fail to comply with these requirements, you risk incurring fines, being taken to court, and having your business's image damaged.

To ensure the security of your QuickBooks Online data, here are some best practices to follow:

Use strong passwords and two-factor authentication

When you set up the passwords for your QuickBooks Online account, you should pick a password that is both strong and unique, and one that is difficult to guess. Additionally, you should think about setting two-factor authentication, which needs a second form of identity (such as a text message or app notification) in addition to your password in order to log in. This may be accomplished by enabling two-factor authentication.

Limit access to sensitive data

Only those personnel at your company who absolutely require access to QuickBooks Online should have it granted to them. In addition, you should only allow access to sensitive data, such as information on bank accounts and payroll records, to those workers who have a legitimate need for it.

Keep software up-to-date

Check QuickBooks Online and any other software or applications that you use in connection with QuickBooks Online on a regular basis to see if there are any updates or security patches available for the product. These upgrades frequently correct security flaws and may assist in preventing data leaks.

Back up your data

Create backups of your QuickBooks Online data on a regular basis to defend against the possibility of losing data in the event that your system is compromised or becomes inoperable. In addition, as an additional layer of defense, you might think about employing a backup service provided by a third party.

Train employees on data security best practices

Your staff should be made aware of the significance of data security and instructed on the most effective procedures for protecting sensitive information. This can encompass subjects like the administration of passwords, phishing schemes, and social engineering assaults.

Security Features of QuickBooks Online

QuickBooks Online incorporates a number of different security elements into its architecture, each of which works together to keep your data as secure as possible. The following is a list of some of the safety features that are available to you in QuickBooks Online:

Data Encryption

QuickBooks Online protects all of the information that you store on the platform by utilizing the most recent advancements in encryption technology. This ensures that none of your private information, including passwords, bank account information, and credit card numbers, may be viewed by anybody who does not have permission to do so. The degree of encryption that is employed by QuickBooks Online is 256 bits, which is the same level of encryption that is used by many banks and other financial organizations.

User Access Control

QuickBooks Online gives you the ability to manage who may access your data and when. You have the ability to provide other individuals varying degrees of access to your data, based on the position they play and the obligations they are responsible for. You can, for instance, prevent specific users from accessing particular sections of the platform or restrict the capacity of those individuals to make modifications to the data you have.

Multi-Factor Authentication

Users of QuickBooks Online have their identities validated by using a multi-factor authentication process. This indicates that users are needed to submit not one but two different kinds of authentication before they are allowed to access their account. It's possible, for instance, that customers may be asked to enter both a password and a verification number that would be transmitted to their cell phones.

Automatic Data Backups

QuickBooks Online will provide daily automated backups of any data you store there. Because of this, you won't need to be concerned about the possibility of your data being lost in the event that the system has an error or some type of catastrophe. In the event that something goes wrong, it will not be difficult for you to restore your data from the backup.

Audit Trail

You are able to monitor any changes made to your data thanks to the audit trail tool that is included in QuickBooks Online. Because of this, it will not be difficult for you to determine who made modifications to your data and when those changes were made. This function is very helpful for companies that need to monitor their financial activities as well as other essential data.

Security Updates

The security elements of QuickBooks Online receive frequent upgrades to guarantee that they are always up to date and functioning properly. Because these changes are delivered to your account in an automated fashion, you do not need to worry about manually upgrading your security settings in any way.

24/7 Monitoring

QuickBooks Online is equipped with a group of security professionals that are on call around the clock to keep an eye out for any possible vulnerabilities in the platform. In the event that there is a breach of security, it will be possible to immediately resolve the issue before it escalates into a significant concern.

Third-Party Integrations

It is a great tool for small businesses since QuickBooks Online was developed to combine without any difficulty with programs developed by other companies. Integrating QuickBooks Online with other software products can provide you access to additional functionality and assist you in automating a significant number of your company procedures. The following is a list of some instances of integrations with third-party services that are available for QuickBooks Online:

Payment Processors

There are a number of different payment processors that are compatible with QuickBooks Online, including PayPal, Stripe, and Square. You will be able to automatically record payments and reconcile your accounts if you integrate your payment processor with QuickBooks Online.

Inventory Management

Integration with a variety of inventory management platforms, including TradeGecko and SOS Inventory, is available for users of QuickBooks Online. By automatically keeping track of inventory levels and issuing purchase orders, these connections can make it easier for you to manage your inventory in an effective manner.

Time Tracking

Integration is available for QuickBooks Online with a number of different time tracking programs, including TSheets and Harvest. Because of these linkages, you will be able to keep better track of the time that employees put in, and the information will be automatically sent to your payroll system.

Customer Relationship Management (CRM)

There are a number of customer relationship management (CRM) programs that can be linked with QuickBooks Online, including Salesforce and Zoho CRM. By synchronizing customer data in an automated fashion and delivering insightful information regarding client behavior, these connections can assist you in more efficiently managing your customer interactions.

E-commerce Platforms

There are a number of e-commerce systems that can be integrated with QuickBooks Online, including Shopify and WooCommerce. You'll be able to more effectively manage your online sales with the assistance of these connections, which sync your sales data and inventory levels automatically.

Expense Management

QuickBooks Online is compatible with a number of other tools for managing expenses, including Expensify and Receipt Bank, among others. These connections can assist you in managing your spending in a more effective manner by automatically importing data pertaining to your expenses and classifying those charges.

Document Management

It is possible to combine QuickBooks Online with a number of different document management services, including Box and Dropbox. The automated synchronization of documents and the provision of encrypted access to files are two ways in which these connections might facilitate more effective document management on your part.

You may improve the efficiency of your company's operations, save time and money, and integrate QuickBooks Online with these and other third-party programs by following these steps. You should be able to automate a significant number of your company procedures with the assistance of these integrations, which will also help you eliminate mistakes and enhance accuracy. In addition, QuickBooks Online features an API (Application Programming Interface), which enables third-party developers to build bespoke connections with the platform. This results in a greater degree of adaptability as well as more customization choices.

rafapress/Depositphotos.com

Chapter 2

Understanding QuickBooks Online

QuickBooks Online is a strong tool that may assist owners of small businesses in more successfully managing their businesses' financial affairs. However, getting a grasp on how to utilize the program may be difficult, particularly for those who are just starting out in the world of bookkeeping or accounting. This chapter will give an in-depth introduction to QuickBooks Online, walking you through the process of establishing your account, managing transactions, and creating reports, among other things. You will have a strong grasp of how QuickBooks Online works by the time you reach the conclusion of this chapter, as well as how to utilize it to improve the financial situation of your company. This chapter will help you get the most out of QuickBooks Online, whether you are just getting started or are trying to simplify your accounting procedures.

Getting Started with QuickBooks Online

It is simple to get started with QuickBooks Online, and the program provides a step-by-step instruction to assist you in setting up your account and getting started with your bookkeeping tasks.

Creating an Account and Setting Up Your Company Profile

The first thing you need to do in order to get started with QuickBooks Online is to sign up for an account with the service. You have the option of signing up for a free trial, which, if activated, will provide you access to the full capabilities of the program for a period of one month. The trial may be engaged at any time within the program's normal business hours. When the trial period has expired, you will be given the opportunity to pick a payment plan that is suitable for the specifications of your business. The numerous levels of service that are available to be bought via QuickBooks Online's various pricing plans are referred to as Simple Start, Essentials, Plus, and Advanced respectively.

After you have successfully registered for an account, the next step is to establish a profile for your company. This profile will include information about your company. You will be required to provide vital information about your company, such as the name of your business, its location, and your contact information, in order to proceed with this. You will also be needed to submit your tax identity number, which will be used in the process of computing your taxes and producing tax records for you. If you do not input your tax identification number, the procedure will not be able to proceed.

How to Navigate the Dashboard, as well as the Menu Options

You will be sent to the dashboard of QuickBooks Online as soon as the configuration of your business profile is complete. By presenting information such as the balances of your bank accounts, outstanding invoices, and expenditure transactions, the dashboard provides you with an overall view of the financial condition of your firm. This helps you make better business decisions.

You have the flexibility to customize the dashboard so that it presents the information that is most pertinent to you, and the menu choices that are situated at the top of the screen may be used to go to other parts of the program. The dashboard can be customized to show the information that is most important to you.

The following is a list of some of the selections that may be made from the menu: Taxes, Sales, and Expenses, as well as Banking and Reports. The program is structured in such a manner that each component is designed to provide assistance to you in the management of a certain aspect of the financial operations of your business. For example, the Sales area helps you to issue and manage invoices, while the Expenses section enables you to keep track of the bills and expenditures that have been made by your firm. Both of these sections may be accessed from the main menu.

Setting Up and Customizing Your Chart of Accounts

Creating your chart of accounts is one of the most crucial steps in getting your QuickBooks Online account set up and running properly. A chart of accounts is a list of all the accounts that your company uses to manage its finances, such as revenue accounts, spending accounts, and asset accounts. These accounts are listed in a certain order called a chart of accounts. QuickBooks Online comes with a default chart of accounts, but you have the option to modify it to better meet the requirements of your company.

You may set up and personalize your chart of accounts by going to the Accounting area of the menu and then selecting Chart of Accounts from the list of available options. You may add new accounts, amend current accounts, and classify your accounts from that location, all of which can assist you in keeping a closer eye on your financial situation.

Chart of Accounts

The chart of accounts is an important component of QuickBooks Online, and its primary function is to provide users with assistance in the methodical organization of the financial data that they keep track of in their businesses. It is a list of all of the accounts that a firm uses in order to keep track of its activities. This is the most fundamental version of an accounting ledger. The assets, liabilities, equity, income, and expenses that have been documented are included here.

One of the many reasons why the chart of accounts is so important is that it provides a basis for recording financial transactions. This is one of the reasons why the chart of accounts is so important. The creation of a chart of accounts gives organizations the ability to ensure that they consistently record transactions in the same fashion by providing them with a blueprint to follow. As a result, it will be much easier to handle and analyze financial data throughout the course of time as a result of this.

When generating a chart of accounts in QuickBooks Online, there are a few fundamental factors that must be kept in mind at all times. These considerations are required to be kept in mind at all times. To get things rolling, it's important to give each of your accounts a name that is not only easy to remember but also conveys some kind of message. As a result of this change, identifying certain accounts in the process of recording transactions will be a lot less complicated.

In addition, it is of the utmost importance to arrange the chart of accounts in a fashion that is coherent with the financial goals of the organization as well as the criteria for financial reporting. For instance, if the firm gets money from a number of sources, it may be helpful to create different income accounts for each source so that it is simpler to monitor the amount of money coming in from each source. This is because having separate income accounts for each source makes it easier to track the total amount of money coming in from each source.

It is possible to make adjustments to the chart of accounts in QuickBooks Online so that it meets the unique needs of the business. This is an extremely useful piece of equipment. This includes the ability to create new accounts, change the names of existing accounts, and reorganize the display of accounts in the list.

A functional chart of accounts must also make use of account numbers, which is another essential component of this kind of accounting document. Having account numbers may be extremely advantageous when it comes to organizing accounts into different categories and making it easier to identify specific accounts when recording financial activities. On the other hand, the use of these services is entirely optional, thus some businesses may choose not to take use of them.

In general, the chart of accounts is an essential part of QuickBooks Online that helps businesses to better organize their monetary data and ensures that they are continually recording transactions in a methodical manner. This is made possible by the fact that QuickBooks Online allows users to create their own charts of accounts. Establishing and maintaining a clear, well-organized, and complete chart of accounts may help businesses make it easier to handle and analyze the financial data they collect over time. This can be a significant benefit to these processes.

Transactions

Transactions are the individual financial events that a business records in QuickBooks Online in order to keep track of its income, expenditures, assets, and liabilities. In other words, transactions are the building blocks of a company's accounting system. To put it another way, transactions are the fundamental components that make up the overall financial picture of an organization. The phrases "sales" and "purchases" as well as "payments," "invoices," and "bills" are all instances of transactions.

When you use QuickBooks Online to keep track of your transactions, one of the most major advantages of using this software is that it gives you the option to simply automate a large chunk of the process. This is one of the reasons why using this program is so beneficial. For instance, when an organization creates an invoice, QuickBooks Online may instantly record the transaction in the appropriate account and give a reminder for when the payment is due. This is possible because QuickBooks Online is cloud-based. In a similar vein, whenever an organization makes a purchase, QuickBooks Online has the capacity of instantly recording the transaction in the appropriate cost account.

Before being able to record a transaction using QuickBooks Online, the user is required to first pick the appropriate kind of transaction from a list of available choices. This must be done before the transaction can be recorded. The user may, for example, pick "sales receipt" or "invoice" from the list of accessible alternatives in order to maintain track of a transaction by selecting one of these options from the available options. Following the selection of the kind of transaction, the user is then given the opportunity to enter the particulars of the transaction. The amount, the date, information about the client or the seller, and any remarks that are relevant to the transaction are all included here.

It is crucial to the operation of this feature that users have the ability to connect transactions that are recorded in the transaction tracking section of QuickBooks Online to specific accounts in the chart of accounts. Because of this, it is much simpler for businesses to keep track of their income and expenditures and to generate financial reports based on the data that they have gathered.

The transaction tracking capabilities of QuickBooks Online comes with a number of useful tools, one of which is the ability to create rules in order to automate certain parts of the process. This is just one of the many helpful tools that comes with this functionality. For instance, a corporation may devise a rule in order to attach a certain expense account to each and every transaction that was conducted with a particular supplier by using the company's accounting software. This would guarantee that every spending was accurately recorded and accounted for. This may lead to a reduction in the amount of time spent inputting data as well as an improvement in accuracy.

In addition, QuickBooks Online makes it possible for companies to choose from a variety of reporting options, which allows them to do a more in-depth analysis of the data associated with their transactions. This includes financial statements such as balance sheets, income statements, and statements of cash flow, in addition to individualized reports that may be modified to meet the specific needs of the business.

When using QuickBooks Online, transactions are an integral part of the larger process of gathering all of the relevant financial data. If the transactions that a company engages in are documented in a consistent and trustworthy way, the company will be able to get beneficial insights into its current state of financial health and make informed choices about its operations. With the support of the automation features and reporting tools offered by QuickBooks Online, companies of any size are able to make the process of tracking transactions into one that is both easier and more productive.

Postmodernstudio/Depositphotos.com

Bank Feeds

Bank feeds are a feature of QuickBooks Online that enables companies to link their bank accounts to the program and automatically import transaction data. This function is helpful for organizations that handle a high volume of financial transactions. This removes the necessity for manually entering data, which not only saves time but also minimizes the likelihood of making mistakes. In this part, we will go through bank feeds in great detail, covering topics such as how to configure them and how to get the most of using them.

Setting Up Bank Feeds

To set up bank feeds in QuickBooks Online, you will need to follow a few simple steps:

- Go to the Banking tab on the left-hand side of the screen.
- Click on Add Account.
- Search for your bank by name or enter your bank's website address.
- Enter your bank account login information.
- Review and categorize transactions.

Once you have set up bank feeds, QuickBooks Online will automatically import transaction data from your bank account. You can then review and categorize the transactions, which will help you keep track of your expenses and income.

Using Bank Feeds Effectively

To get the most out of bank feeds, there are a few best practices you should follow:

- Review your transactions regularly: It's important to review your transactions regularly to ensure that they are correctly categorized and that there are no errors.

- Categorize transactions correctly: Make sure you are categorizing transactions correctly to ensure that your financial reports are accurate.

- Use rules to categorize transactions automatically: QuickBooks Online allows you to set up rules to categorize transactions automatically. This can save time and ensure that transactions are consistently categorized.

- Reconcile your bank accounts regularly: Reconciling your bank accounts regularly is important to ensure that your records match those of your bank.

Benefits of Using Bank Feeds

Using bank feeds in QuickBooks Online offers several benefits:

- Time savings: Bank feeds eliminate the need for manual data entry, which saves time.

- Reduced errors: Manual data entry can lead to errors, which can be costly. Bank feeds reduce the risk of errors.

- Accurate records: Using bank feeds ensures that your records are accurate and up-to-date.

- Improved cash flow management: Bank feeds provide real-time visibility into your cash flow, which can help you make better business decisions.

Reports

QuickBooks Online offers a broad variety of reports that can assist owners of small businesses in gaining a better understanding of the company's overall financial health. The information that may be gleaned from reports may include cash flow, costs, income, and perhaps more. In this part, we will go through the many reports that may be generated using QuickBooks Online, as well as the steps necessary to do so.

Profit and Loss Report

A company's income, cost of products sold, and costs are detailed in the Profit and Loss Report, which is often referred to as an Income Statement. This report covers a certain time period. When determining whether or not a company is profitable, this report is absolutely necessary. Simply navigate to the Reports page in QuickBooks Online and click on the Profit and Loss option once you're there. This will produce a Profit and Loss Report.

Balance Sheet Report

A snapshot of a company's financial status at a certain point in time may be seen in the Balance Sheet Report. It outlines the assets, liabilities, and equity of the company. The information contained in this report is helpful for gaining an idea of the financial health and liquidity of a firm. Simply navigate to the Reports tab in QuickBooks Online and click on the Balance Sheet option once you're there. This will produce a Balance Sheet Report.

Cash Flow Statement

A company's Cash Flow Statement will detail the cash that came into and went out of the company during a certain time period. This report is helpful for assessing the cash situation of a firm as well as the organization's capacity to satisfy its financial obligations. Simply navigate to the Reports tab in QuickBooks Online and click on Cash Flow Statement to get a Cash Flow Statement for your business.

Accounts Receivable Aging Report

The Accounts Receivable Aging Report provides information on an organization's unpaid bills as well as the length of time that these invoices have been overdue. This report is helpful for determining which clients are late with their payments and tracking overall cash flow. Simply navigate to the Reports tab in QuickBooks Online and click on the Accounts Receivable Aging option when you want to produce an Accounts Receivable Aging Report.

Accounts Payable Aging Report

The Accounts Payable Aging Report provides insight into a company's overdue debts as well as the length of time those bills have remained unpaid. The cash flow and the timely payment of bills may both be managed more effectively with the help of this report. Simply navigate to the Reports tab in QuickBooks Online and click on the Accounts Payable Aging option when you want to produce an Accounts Payable Aging Report.

Sales by Product/Service Summary Report

A company's sales may be broken down into individual products or services using the Sales by Product/Service Summary Report. This report is helpful for determining which goods or services are selling well and which ones are not selling as well as they could be. Simply navigate to the Reports tab in QuickBooks Online and click on the Sales by Product/Service Summary option there. This will allow you to build a Sales by Product/Service Summary Report.

Sales by Customer Summary Report

A company's sales are broken down into individual customers in the Sales by Customer Summary Report. This report is helpful for determining which clients are producing the most money as well as locating prospects for expansion. Simply navigate to the Reports tab in QuickBooks Online and click the Sales by Customer Summary option there. This will produce a Sales by Customer Summary Report.

Budget vs Actuals Report

The Budget vs Actuals Report compares the actual financial outcomes of a firm with the amounts that were budgeted for that company. This report is helpful for assessing performance in relation to the budget as well as highlighting areas in which actual results are notably different from the amounts that were planned for. Simply navigate to the Reports tab in QuickBooks Online and click on the Budget versus Actuals drop-down menu to get a Budget vs Actuals Report.

Collaboration and User Management

QuickBooks Online has capabilities that are vital for businesses, particularly those with several workers or accounting experts who need access to the company's financial data. These features include user management and collaboration, both of which are essential for such enterprises. QuickBooks Online enables business owners to provide other users, such as bookkeepers, accountants, and financial advisers, with access to the system so that they may perform their jobs. Additionally, it offers a variety of collaboration tools, including as user authorization, work delegation, and messaging, which serve to expedite accounting procedures and increase communication among members of the team.

User Management

QuickBooks Online enables business owners to share their company's financial data with other users, so that other people may view or manage it. It is possible that the user will have access to a variety of various features and functions inside QuickBooks Online according to the role that has been granted to them. The following are the most prevalent roles:

- Master Administrator: This role has full access to all features of QuickBooks Online and can manage other users, company settings, and bank accounts.

- Company Administrator: This role can manage other users, company settings, and bank accounts, but does not have access to sensitive financial information.

- Standard User: This role can access all the basic features of QuickBooks Online, such as creating invoices, expenses, and other transactions, but cannot access sensitive financial information.

- Reports Only: This role can only access financial reports and cannot make any changes to the financial data.

Users can be added or removed at any time, and their access to QuickBooks Online can be modified to fit their role in the company.

Collaboration Features

QuickBooks Online offers several collaboration features that can help improve communication and streamline accounting processes. Here are some of the key features:

- User Permissions: Business owners can set up permissions for users, which determines which features and functions they can access within QuickBooks Online. This can help to prevent unauthorized access to sensitive financial information.

- Task Delegation: Business owners can delegate tasks to specific users within QuickBooks Online. For example, a business owner can assign a task to a bookkeeper to reconcile bank accounts or to an accountant to prepare tax returns.

- Messaging: QuickBooks Online has a messaging feature that allows team members to communicate with each other directly within the system. This can help to keep all communication in one place and ensure that everyone is on the same page

- File Sharing: Business owners can share files such as receipts, invoices, and other financial documents with other team members within QuickBooks Online. This can help to streamline the process of collecting and organizing financial data.

- Activity Log: QuickBooks Online has an activity log that tracks all user activity within the system. This can help business owners to monitor user activity and ensure that there is no unauthorized access to sensitive financial information.

Chapter 3

Advantages and Disadvantages of QuickBooks Online

As the owner of a small business, making the appropriate option about the accounting software to use for your company is an important decision that may have an effect on the success of your company. QuickBooks Online is a well-known cloud-based accounting software that provides a multitude of advantages, including adaptability, accessibility, and connectivity with many other company applications. On the other hand, just like any other piece of software, it comes with a few limitations, the most notable of which are its restricted feature set in comparison to desktop software and its possible vulnerability to security breaches.

This chapter will discuss the pros and cons of utilizing QuickBooks Online, as well as provide a comparison with desktop software. You'll be able to make an educated conclusion about whether or not QuickBooks Online is the appropriate accounting software for your company if you take the time to familiarize yourself with both its positive and negative aspects.

Advantages of QuickBooks Online

QuickBooks Online, often known as QBO, is accounting software that is hosted in the cloud and gives proprietors of small businesses a broad variety of benefits. The following is a list of some of the most major advantages of utilizing QBO:

Accessibility and Convenience

The ease of access and convenience that come along with using QBO is one of the most major benefits that it offers. Because it is hosted in the cloud, users may access their financial data and carry out accounting chores from any location and at any time, provided they have an internet connection. This is especially helpful for owners of small businesses who are frequently on the go or who need to access their financial data while working remotely.

Integration with Other Business Tools

It is meant to interact with a broad variety of other business tools, including software for processing payments and payroll, as well as software for managing projects. This enables customers to more quickly link QBO to the technologies they already use, which in turn helps them optimize their operations. Connecting Quick Books Online (QBO) to payment processing software such as Stripe or PayPal, for instance, enables users to instantly import sales data into QBO, therefore eliminating the need for human data entry and the likelihood of making mistakes.

Customization and Scalability

For companies of any size, QBO may be tailored to fulfill specific requirements because to its high level of adaptability and scalability. Users have access to a selection of different price plans, which they may select from based on the services they want and the size of their respective companies. Users are able to modify the program to meet the requirements of their particular companies by taking advantage of the many

customization options that are made available by QBO.
These possibilities include the generation of bespoke
invoices and reports.

Real-Time Financial Data

Users of QBO have access to real-time financial data,
which may be very helpful for small business owners
that need to make choices quickly. Users are able to
access their financial data in real time, giving them the
ability to remain on top of their finances and make
decisions based on accurate information. Examples of
this type of data include income statements, balance
sheets, and cash flow statements.

Automatic Backup and Security

QBO reduces the likelihood of user data being lost as a
result of hardware failure or other catastrophic events by
performing automated backups and storing them in a
safe manner on remote servers. In addition, the user data
stored in QBO is protected from illegal access and other
types of cyber threats by sophisticated security measures

provided by QBO. These features include multi-factor authentication and encryption.

User-Friendly Interface

The UI of QBO is designed to be intuitive and straightforward, making it simple to use even for non-accounting professionals and owners of small businesses. Without substantial accounting expertise or training, users are able to effortlessly navigate the program and do accounting chores such as issuing invoices, monitoring spending, and reconciling bank accounts. This eliminates the need for users to hire an accountant.

Cost-Effective

When compared to traditional desktop accounting software, Quick Books Online (QBO) is often more cost-effective since it has fewer initial expenses and does not require the upgrading or maintenance of any hardware. In addition, customers have the option of selecting from a number of different price plans, making it simple for them to discover a plan that is suitable for both their financial situation and the requirements of their company.

In general, QuickBooks Online provides small company owners with a number of benefits, including accessibility, connectivity with other business tools, customization, real-time financial data, automated backup and security, a user-friendly interface, and cost-effectiveness. Some of these benefits are listed below. By taking advantage of these benefits, owners of small businesses may simplify their accounting procedures and improve their ability to make decisions that will contribute to the expansion of their companies.

Disadvantages of QuickBooks Online

Users of QuickBooks Online should be aware of a few drawbacks, despite the fact that the software has a great many benefits to provide in its favor. It is essential to have a full comprehension of these drawbacks before arriving at a conclusion, despite the fact that none of them are serious enough to call into question the reliability of the program. The following is a list of some of the drawbacks of using QuickBooks Online:

Internet Dependency

The fact that QuickBooks Online cannot function without constant access to the internet is among the service's most significant drawbacks. This implies that customers are unable to access their QuickBooks Online account if they do not have an internet connection, and if the internet connection is not strong enough, it might be tough to operate with the program in an effective manner. Users are also responsible for ensuring the safety of their internet connection in order to safeguard any sensitive financial data they may have.

Limited Functionality

The desktop edition of QuickBooks offers more capabilities than the online version of QuickBooks does. Batch invoicing, batch transactions, and other complex functions are only available in the desktop version of QuickBooks, so while QuickBooks Online does give customers with the core features they need to manage their accounts, it is missing some of the more advanced features present in the desktop edition. This might be a big detriment for companies who operate in an industry that requires the use of more complex features.

Cost

Although QuickBooks Online is a cost-effective choice for one to consider for one's small business, it has the potential to become more expensive as the company expands. The customer may demand higher-priced plans as their needs expand, which might result in a large rise in the overall cost of utilizing QuickBooks Online. In addition, the cost of QuickBooks Online can be greater than the cost of the desktop edition, particularly for customers who choose to buy the desktop program outright rather than pay a monthly subscription fee. This is especially true for users who want to pay for the desktop software.

Data Security

Even though QuickBooks Online includes extensive security protections, there is always a possibility of a data breach, particularly if users don't take the appropriate procedures to protect their information. To lower the likelihood of a data breach occurring, users are obligated to take precautions such as employing robust passwords, enabling two-factor authentication, and protecting their login credentials at all times.

Learning Curve

The learning curve for QuickBooks Online is a little bit steep, particularly for first-time customers who are not very experienced with accounting software. The program is simple to operate once the user is familiar with its capabilities; nonetheless, it may take some practice for the user to become proficient in its use. Users who don't have the time to invest in learning how to use the program properly can find this to be a big downside of the product.

Comparison of QuickBooks Online and Desktop Software

One of the answers that is regarded to be the most dependable and widely used piece of accounting software that is now available on the market is QuickBooks. QuickBooks is a well-known name in the world of accounting software, and it can be obtained in two distinct formats: online and on a traditional desktop computer. Each version has its own unique set of traits, in addition to a set of advantages and disadvantages that are exclusive to that variety. This section's objective is to present you with a comparison of the two versions of QuickBooks and to aid you in picking the version of the software that is best suited for your business.

Intuit originally became well-known in the software market with the release of QuickBooks Desktop, which has been in operation for more than 20 years at this point. QuickBooks Desktop is software that is locally installed, which means that it is installed on your computer and can be accessed directly from your computer. Additionally, this kind of software is referred to as "desktop" version of QuickBooks. Because it was installed on your local machine, you may use it even if you do not have an online connection. On the other hand, QuickBooks Online is a piece of software that is run on servers that are located in the cloud. This signifies that it is accessed via a connection to the internet, and that it is also available from any place and on any device.

Features Comparison

The feature set is one of the most major areas in which QuickBooks Online and Desktop differ significantly from one another. QuickBooks Desktop provides users with access to a broader range of functionality and configuration choices than its online counterpart, QuickBooks Online. For example, QuickBooks Desktop provides industry-specific editions such as QuickBooks Pro, Premier, and Enterprise, but QuickBooks Online does not provide such options. On the other hand, QuickBooks Online provides access to more advanced capabilities, such as automated bank feeds, cloud storage, and mobile access, none of which are accessible in the desktop version of QuickBooks.

Accessibility and Usability

When compared to QuickBooks Desktop, QuickBooks Online is far easier to access and more intuitive to utilize.

On the other hand, QuickBooks Desktop can only be accessed from the device on which it was originally installed, but QuickBooks Online may be accessed from any location so long as there is an internet connection. The UI of QuickBooks Online is more intuitive and user-friendly, which makes it simpler for novice users to browse and use the program.

Security and Data Backup

When it comes to protection, both the online and desktop versions of QuickBooks come with their own unique set of safety features. Your data is encrypted using 128-bit SSL technology while it is stored in the cloud by QuickBooks Online. On the other hand, QuickBooks Desktop maintains your data on your local computer, which makes it susceptible to security flaws such as theft and loss of data. QuickBooks Online will also perform automated backups of your data, so guaranteeing that your data is kept in a safe and secure environment at all times.

Cost Comparison

When compared to QuickBooks Online, the initial investment for QuickBooks Desktop is more significant. Users of QuickBooks Desktop must pay a one-time fee in order to use the software, and they must update to the newest version of the program every few years. On the other hand, QuickBooks Online is a subscription service that users pay for on either a monthly or yearly basis. QuickBooks Online may appear to be more expensive over time; however, it really provides greater flexibility and may be more cost-effective for smaller firms.

Customer Support

In comparison to QuickBooks Desktop, the customer assistance available through QuickBooks Online is superior. In contrast to QuickBooks Desktop, which only offers customer help during business hours, QuickBooks Online's support is available through phone, email, or live chat around the clock, every day of the year.

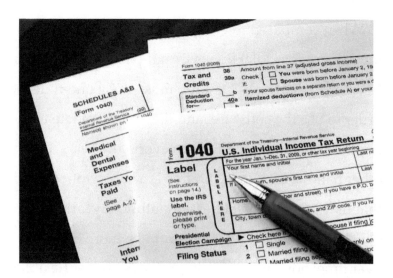

johnkwan/Depositphotos.com

Scan the QR code

and get

your bonus

Chapter 4

Getting Started with QuickBooks Online

In order to make the most out of QuickBooks Online, it is important to understand how to get started. This chapter will provide a step-by-step guide on how to set up your QuickBooks Online account, enter your company information, and customize your settings. By the end of this chapter, you will be ready to start using QuickBooks Online to manage your business finances efficiently and effectively.

Creating a QuickBooks Online Account

The first thing you need to do in order to begin using QuickBooks Online is to sign up for an account on their website. It is a straightforward procedure that may be finished in a matter of a few minutes. In this part we'll go through the procedures that you need to follow in order to establish an account for QuickBooks Online.

Step 1: Choose a Subscription Plan

Your first order of business is to select a payment strategy for your membership. There are four distinct subscription options available to choose from while using QuickBooks Online: Simple Start, Essentials, Plus, and Advanced. The pricing and feature complements that come with each tier of service are distinct. On the QuickBooks Online website, you may review each plan's feature set as well as its cost to make an informed decision about which plan best suits your needs.

Step 2: Create an Account

After making your choice of subscription plan, you can start the process of setting up your account by going to the QuickBooks Online website and selecting the "Sign Up" option from the menu that appears there. You will be prompted to supply some fundamental information, such as your name, email address, and a password, among other things. Be careful to pick a secure password by using a combination of several types of characters, including capital and lowercase letters, digits, and special characters.

Step 3: Enter Business Information

After you have made your account, you will be prompted to input some fundamental details regarding your company, such as the name of your company, its address, and its telephone number. You will also be prompted to select the nature of your company and the sector it operates in. The information that you provide will be used to tailor your QuickBooks Online account to meet your particular requirements.

Step 4: Set Up Bank Accounts

The following thing you need to do is link your bank accounts to QuickBooks Online. This makes it possible for you to effortlessly import your transactions and monitor your accounts at the same time. In order to connect your bank accounts, you will be required to give the login credentials for each of your banks. QuickBooks Online employs security on par with that of a bank to safeguard and secure the information you enter.

Step 5: Customize Your Settings

After you have linked your bank accounts, you will be able to modify your settings to better suit your preferences and requirements. This involves the creation of your chart of accounts, profiles for both customers and vendors, as well as the configuration of your goods and services.

Step 6: Start Using QuickBooks Online

You are free to begin using QuickBooks Online to manage your business's finances now that your account has been established. The dashboard gives you an overall picture of your current financial condition, allows you to examine your transactions, and allows you to produce reports. In addition, QuickBooks Online enables you to manage your inventory, track your costs, and make invoices for your business.

Navigating QuickBooks Online

In this section, we are going to discuss how to navigate through the several screens that comprise the user interface of QuickBooks Online. QuickBooks Online has a user interface that is both clear and intuitive, making it possible for users to do a wide range of tasks in a stress-free and simple manner.

The "dashboard" is the name of the principal screen that appears once you have successfully logged into your QuickBooks Online account for the very first time. By using this menu, you will be able to get access to a broad range of the program's features as well as its possibilities. The dashboard is composed of a number of different sections that, when put together, provide a condensed overview of the current financial situation facing your organization. The terms "Bank Accounts," "Sales," "Expenses," and "Profit and Loss" are all examples of modules that fall under this category.

Another essential component of QuickBooks Online is the left navigation panel, which can be found in the program. It provides rapid access to a broad number of products and services, some of which include customers, suppliers, reports, and settings, amongst other things. You have another choice available to you in the form of a search box, which allows you to look for a certain feature or function of the website.

On the main page, you will see a record of all of your recent activity, including a list of your most recent transactions as well as reminders and notifications. The first screen you see while using the application is this one. You have the power to make the home screen unique to you by customizing it so that it only shows the information that is relevant to you.

You have the option of making use of the Quick Create menu, which can be accessed by clicking on the plus sign (+) icon that can be found in the top right hand corner of the screen. You will now be able to access a certain feature or function that is offered in QuickBooks Online as a result of doing so. You will be able to produce new transactions, such as invoices, estimates, bills, and purchase orders, by using this menu.

Not just via the Quick Create menu, but also through the main menu, you have access to a broad range of features and functions that may be used in the program. To access the primary menu, just locate the icon in the top left corner of the screen that resembles three horizontal lines crossing each other, and then click on that icon. From this section, you will have access to a number of services, including Customers, Vendors, Expenses, Reports, and Settings, among others.

In addition, the user interface of QuickBooks Online may be altered to be more suitable for your needs if you so want. You have the opportunity to adjust the home screen, as well as rearrange the modules on the dashboard, add or remove shortcuts from the left navigation panel, and more. In addition, you may change the order in which the modules appear on the dashboard.

Postmodernstudio/Depositphotos.com

Setting up Your Company Profile

After you have established your QuickBooks Online account and been accustomed to the software's interface, the next step is to build a profile for your business in QuickBooks Online. The company profile that you create for your QuickBooks Online account serves as the platform around which everything else is built. It contains all of the key information about your firm, which will be used to produce reports, invoices, and other crucial papers in the future. In the following part, we will discuss the procedures that must be followed in order to create a profile for the company in QuickBooks Online.

Step 1: Navigate to the Company Settings

Simply choose the Gear symbol that is found in the upper right hand corner of the screen to get started on configuring your business profile. This action will open up the Settings menu for QuickBooks Online. To access your account settings, select the "Account and Settings" option from this menu.

Step 2: Enter Your Company Information

When you have successfully navigated to the "Account and Settings" menu, you will see that there is a list of tabs located on the left-hand side of the screen. To gain access to the business information settings, select the "Company" option from the navigation menu. You will be able to input the name of your firm, as well as its address, telephone number, email address, and website, in this section.

You have the option of entering information pertaining to your business's kind, industry, and taxes, in addition to the fundamental details of your organization. Because this data will be used to produce crucial reports and other documents, it is critical that you enter it as properly as possible.

Step 3: Customize Your Invoices

You may also personalize your invoices by clicking on the "Company" page and going there. This involves adding the logo of your organization, choosing a color scheme, and writing a personalized message to your consumers.

Not only does customizing your invoices give them a more professional appearance, but it also guarantees that your branding is maintained consistently throughout all of the papers that are shown to your customers.

Step 4: Set Up Payment Processing

The "Payments" page of the "Account and Settings" menu in QuickBooks Online provides access to a number of different payment processing options, all of which may be configured by the user. You have the option to take payments by PayPal, credit cards, and wire transfers, among other methods.

The processing of payments is a vital step that must be taken in order to get paid in a timely and effective manner. You can guarantee that your clients have an easy method to pay you by providing a number of different payment alternatives for them to choose from.

Step 5: Set Up Sales Tax

If you are obligated to collect sales tax for your company, you may configure your sales tax rates under the "Taxes" tab of the "Account and Settings" menu if you have access to that menu. Your sales tax is automatically computed by QuickBooks Online depending on the tax rates that apply to your business and the location of your consumers.

Setting up your sales tax in QuickBooks Online guarantees that you are collecting the appropriate amount of sales tax and can help you prevent any compliance concerns that may arise as a result of failing to do so.

Step 6: Add Team Members

Under the "Team" tab of the "Account and Settings" menu, you will find the option to add members to a team if you intend to collaborate with other people. This enables you to offer members of your team access to your QuickBooks Online account and assign varying levels of access to them based on the responsibilities they are responsible for.

Bringing on new members to your team can assist you in streamlining your workflow and ensuring that all individuals have access to the information they require to successfully complete their tasks.

Adding Customers and Vendors

When first beginning to build up your company's financial records in QuickBooks Online, one of the most important steps is to add customers and vendors. Customers and vendors are the persons or organizations with whom your company conducts financial transactions, such as making sales or purchases, and are referred to as "customers" and "vendors," respectively. In order to have an accurate and up-to-date record of the financial operations of your company, it is very necessary to input information about your customers and vendors into QuickBooks Online in an accurate manner.

Adding a Customer

To begin the process of adding a customer in QuickBooks Online, first choose the Customers tab located in the menu on the left side of the screen. To become a new customer, select the "New Customer" button from that menu. You will be presented with a form into which you may put the name of the customer, their contact information, and the payment arrangements. You also have the option of adding supplementary information, such as the customer's billing address, shipping address, and tax information. After you have completed entering all of the required information, you can add the client to your list by clicking the "Save" button.

Adding a Vendor

In QuickBooks Online, go to the left-hand menu and select the Vendors tab to add a new vendor to your business. To create a new vendor account, use the "New Vendor" option. You will be presented with a form in which you may input the name of the seller, their contact information, and the payment terms. You also have the option of including supplementary particulars, such as the tax information, billing address, and shipping address of the vendor. After you have completed entering all of the required information, you can add the vendor to your list by clicking the "Save" button.

Managing Customer and Vendor Information

After you have imported customers and vendors into QuickBooks Online, you will be able to manage the information associated with them from the tabs that are specific to each group. You may examine a list of all of your customers and their details by clicking on the Customers page. This list will include information about your customers' outstanding amounts, payment histories, and contact information. You have the ability to generate invoices, sales receipts, and credit notes for each individual client straight from inside their customer profile.

You may view a list of all of your vendors and their information, including their outstanding balances, payment history, and contact information, from the Vendors tab. In a similar fashion, you can view a list of all of your suppliers and their information from the Customers tab. You are also able to immediately make purchase orders and bills for each individual vendor from inside their profile.

Integrating Customer and Vendor Information with Transactions

QuickBooks Online has the capability to seamlessly combine information on customers and vendors with transaction records, which is one of the program's most significant features. When you produce an invoice for a client, for instance, QuickBooks Online will immediately retrieve the customer's information from their profile. This will save you time and reduce the likelihood of making a mistake. When you produce a bill for a vendor using QuickBooks Online, the software will automatically retrieve the vendor's information from their profile. This helps to ensure that the bill is accurate.

When it comes to the process of keeping correct financial records for your company, one of the most important steps is using QuickBooks Online to enter and manage information on your customers and vendors. When preparing transactions like invoices and bills, you may limit the number of mistakes and save time if you take the time to check that this information is valid and up to date.

Connecting Bank and Credit Card Accounts

Connecting your bank and credit card accounts to QuickBooks Online is one of the steps that must be taken in order to keep your financial records correct and up to date. Keeping your financial records accurate and up to date involves doing a number of procedures. If you follow those steps, you won't have to key in any of the transaction details or account information by hand, and you'll be able to automatically import transactions and reconcile your accounts. The processes required to connect your bank and credit card accounts to QuickBooks Online are detailed in the following section, and we will guide you through each step step-by-step.

To get started with QuickBooks Online, go to the left-hand menu and choose the Banking option from the drop-down menu. In this section, if you want to link a bank account or credit card account, you may do so by selecting the appropriate option from the drop-down menu. To get started, choose this menu item from the available choices.

After that, you will be given the opportunity to search for your Credit Card Company or financial institution that issued your credit card. If your service provider is shown, you should click on it and then enter your login details for that account when it pops up. If your service provider is displayed, you should click on it. If your vendor is not listed, you have the option of manually inputting transactions in either the CSV or QBO file format, depending on which you prefer.

After you have successfully linked your bank account or credit card account to QuickBooks Online, the program will instantly begin importing your transactions. You may monitor the progress of the importation by clicking on the Transactions tab. It is vital to keep in mind that this process could take some time since the system will have to import all transactions going back to the very beginning of the account's history. This is why keeping this in mind is so important.

When each of your transactions is imported into the system, you will be required to provide appropriate categories to each of those transactions. QuickBooks

Online will make an effort to categorize them based on the kind of transaction, but it is imperative that you review these classifications and make any necessary revisions before proceeding.

In addition, you have the option of automating this process by establishing bank rules that will serve as a guide. You might, for instance, design a rule that would automatically label all transactions with a certain seller as "Office Supplies." This would be done on an automated basis.

Connecting these several kinds of accounts offers a number of key benefits, one of the most notable of which is the capability to reconcile balances held at banking institutions and on credit cards. Comparing the transactions that have been recorded in QuickBooks Online with those that have been recorded on your bank or credit card account is an important step in the process of reconciling your finances. Because of this, there is a greater possibility that the records you keep of your finances will be accurate and up to date.

When you click the Banking tab, a list of accounts will show below it. To reconcile your accounts, choose the account you want to reconcile from this list. Use the "Start Reconciling" button that is found in this area to begin matching your transactions to those that appear on your statement, and then follow the on-screen directions that appear after using the button.

To provide a brief summary, linking your bank and credit card accounts to QuickBooks Online is a vital step in the process of keeping accurate and up-to-date financial records for your organization. It provides you the capacity to automate the import of transactions as well as the categorization of those transactions, and it also grants you the ability to reconcile your accounts so that you can be certain that they are correct.

Setting Up Products and Services

Setting up products and services is a crucial step in QuickBooks Online that helps businesses track their inventory and manage their sales. By setting up products and services in QuickBooks Online, businesses can easily create and send invoices, track sales, and manage their inventory. In this section, we will discuss how to set up products and services in QuickBooks Online.

Setting up Products

To set up products in QuickBooks Online, follow these steps:

- Go to the Gear icon and select Products and Services.
- Click New, and then select Product or Service.
- Enter the product name, SKU (if applicable), and product description.
- Select the income account and the sales tax if applicable.
- Enter the price and select the unit of measure.

Setting up Services

To set up services in QuickBooks Online, follow these steps:

- Go to the Gear icon and select Products and Services.

- Click New, and then select Product or Service.

- Enter the service name and description.

- Select the income account and the sales tax if applicable.

- Enter the rate and select the unit of measure.

Setting up Bundles

Bundles are a group of products or services that are sold together. To set up bundles in QuickBooks Online, follow these steps:

- Go to the Gear icon and select Products and Services.

- Click New, and then select Bundle.

- Enter the bundle name, SKU (if applicable), and description.

- Add the products and services that are included in the bundle.

- Select the sales price for the bundle.

Managing Inventory

QuickBooks Online offers a basic inventory management system that allows businesses to track their inventory levels and costs. To manage inventory in QuickBooks Online, follow these steps:

- Go to the Gear icon and select Products and Services.
- Click on the product that you want to manage.
- Select the Edit icon and then select the checkbox for Track quantity and price/rate.
- Enter the starting quantity and cost for the product.
- When you sell the product, QuickBooks Online will automatically adjust the inventory levels and update the cost of goods sold.

Setting up Categories

Setting up categories in QuickBooks Online can help businesses organize their products and services for reporting purposes. To set up categories in QuickBooks Online, follow these steps:

- Go to the Gear icon and select Products and Services.
- Click on the category that you want to manage.
- Select the Edit icon and then select the checkbox for Is subcategory.
- Enter the parent category if applicable.
- Click Save.

In conclusion, setting up products and services in QuickBooks Online is a crucial step in managing your business finances. By setting up your products and services accurately, you can easily create and send invoices, track sales, manage inventory, and make informed business decisions based on the reporting data provided by QuickBooks Online.

Chapter 5

Exploring QuickBooks Online Features

The purpose of this chapter is to investigate the different functions and capabilities that are available via QuickBooks Online. QuickBooks Online is a strong tool for managing money, and it provides a broad variety of features that may help small company owners simplify their operations and save time. If you manage a small business, you should consider using QuickBooks Online. In this chapter, we will explore some of the most important aspects of QuickBooks Online as well as the ways in which these tools might assist your company.

As part of our commitment to ensuring that you get the most benefit possible from your QuickBooks Online account, we will also give hints and guidance on how to make the most of the capabilities at your disposal. This chapter will thus give vital insights into the various features and functions that are accessible to you, regardless of whether you are just starting out with QuickBooks Online or have been using it for a while.

Managing Sales and Income

Small companies may take use of a wide range of tools provided by QuickBooks Online to better manage their sales and profits. In the following paragraphs, we will go through these characteristics in further depth.

Invoicing

Invoicing is a crucial component for every company that needs to get paid for its goods or services and wants to do it successfully. Creating and sending customer invoices in a professional manner is made simple using QuickBooks Online's invoicing capabilities. You have the option of personalizing the invoices to reflect your brand by adding your company's logo, colors, and design. You can also set up recurring billing for consumers that buy your goods or services on a regular basis by creating recurring invoices in your accounting software.

Payment Processing

Because it is integrated with a number of different payment processors, such as Stripe and PayPal, QuickBooks Online makes it simple to take online payments. For the convenience of your clients, you may make it possible for them to pay their bills online by configuring a payment gateway and then connecting it to their QuickBooks accounts. In addition, you have the option of setting up clients with overdue payments to get automated payment reminders.

Sales Receipts

Receipts of sale are an essential component for companies that transact the purchase of their goods or services in the same physical location as the customer. You are able to generate and print sales receipts, as well as send them to consumers while using QuickBooks Online. You may also add discounts or special promotions to the receipts, as well as personalize them with your company's logo, to entice customers to make more purchases.

Sales Reports

QuickBooks Online gives you access to a variety of sales reports, each of which may provide you with important information about how well your company is doing. Tracking your sales, determining which of your items or services are most popular, and keeping an eye on your customers' spending habits are all things that can be accomplished with the assistance of these reports. You will be able to boost your sales and income by making decisions that are data-driven with the use of this information.

Sales Tax

The administration of sales tax can be a challenging issue for companies operating on a smaller scale. The procedure is made easier by QuickBooks Online, which calculates the applicable sales tax for each transaction depending on the tax settings you have selected. You may also configure multiple tax rates to apply to certain goods and services, and have those rates applied automatically to each transaction.

Deposits

Because QuickBooks Online enables you to record payments received from customers as deposits, the software may assist you in keeping a closer eye on your company's overall cash flow. You have the option to not only record full payments but also partial payments and overpayments, and then apply them to subsequent invoices.

Overall, the sales and revenue management capabilities of QuickBooks Online give small businesses with a comprehensive solution to successfully manage their finances. This is the case because of the comprehensive nature of the service. Because of these capabilities, it is much simpler for businesses to concentrate on expanding their customer base and increasing their profits. These features assist ease the process of invoicing and payment, track sales performance, and handle sales tax.

Managing Expenses and Bills

In order to avoid any kind of financial difficulties, it is essential for you as the owner of a firm to effectively control your spending. QuickBooks Online provides a variety of tools that might assist you in keeping track of your invoices and spending. The software allows you to enter bills, keep track of costs, and pay bills immediately from within the program.

In QuickBooks Online, you may handle your invoices and costs in a few of the following ways:

Entering Bills

In QuickBooks Online, you are able to enter the receipts for the things that you have bought. This will assist you in keeping an eye on your expenditures and ensuring that payments are made on time. To add a bill, select "Bill" from the drop-down menu that appears when you click the "+New" button. Fill in the name of the retailer, the products that were purchased, and the total cost. After the bill has been added, it will show up in the

"Bills" area, where you will also be able to monitor when the payment is due.

Tracking Expenses

Connecting your bank accounts and credit cards to QuickBooks Online gives you the ability to keep track of your expenditures. You are able to assign a category to each transaction and keep track of them individually. This will assist you in determining where your money is going and point you in the direction of areas in which you may reduce your spending. To keep track of your spending, select the "Banking" tab and then click on the "Bank Feeds" button. After that, you'll be able to appropriately classify each transaction.

Paying Bills

You can pay your bills straight from within QuickBooks Online if you have that feature enabled. You may set up automated bill payments for regular costs, at which point the bills will be paid on their own. To pay bills, select "Pay Bills" from the menu that appears when you click the "+New" button. Choose the invoices that you need to pay as well as the bank account that the money will come from to make the payment.

Managing Receipts

In addition, QuickBooks Online enables you to handle receipts by photographing them on your mobile device and then uploading the images to the accounting software. This will assist you in keeping track of your expenditures and ensuring that you do not lose any receipts. To manage your receipts, click the "+New" button and then select the "Receipt" option from the drop-down menu. The image of the receipt may then be uploaded to QuickBooks Online after you have taken a picture of it.

Reports

QuickBooks Online provides you with a variety of reports that will assist you in reviewing your expenditures and invoices. To obtain a comprehensive perspective of the financial health of your company, you may create a statement of profits and losses, a balance sheet, and a statement of cash flow. Go to the "Reports" page and choose the report that you want to produce in order to have access to the reports.

In conclusion, using QuickBooks Online to manage your bills and costs is not only simple but also quite efficient. You will be able to monitor your spending, ensure that your invoices are paid on time, and do financial analysis of your company if you make use of the capabilities listed above.

Managing Inventory

The management of a company's inventory is an essential component of running a successful business, and QuickBooks Online provides a full suite of capabilities designed to assist businesses in effectively managing their inventory.

Businesses are able to maintain inventory levels, analyze product performance, and automate inventory-related tasks thanks to the inventory management function in QuickBooks Online. The following is a list of some of the important elements that are included in QuickBooks On line's inventory management:

Tracking inventory levels

Businesses now have the ability to monitor their stock levels in real time thanks to QuickBooks Online. This enables companies to constantly have an accurate view of the amounts of their inventory, allowing them to prevent stockouts as well as overstocking their supplies.

Setting up inventory items

In QuickBooks Online, a company may create inventory items by adding data such as the item's name, description, stock keeping unit (SKU), and price. This makes it simple to handle things in inventory and keep tabs on how well they are performing.

Creating purchase orders

Businesses are able to generate purchase orders for inventory products through the use of QuickBooks Online. This not only helps companies keep track of their orders, but it also guarantees that they have sufficient inventory to fulfill customer needs.

Receiving inventory

By generating a bill for the business or placing a purchase order, QuickBooks Online makes it simple for companies to take delivery of inventory. This provides an up-to-date view of inventory levels and assists firms in maintaining control over their stock.

Creating sales orders

Businesses are able to generate sales orders for inventory products through the use of QuickBooks Online. This makes it easier for companies to handle their orders and guarantees that they have sufficient inventory to fulfill all of their requests.

Fulfilling orders

In QuickBooks Online, after a sales order has been placed, businesses are able to effortlessly fulfill it by generating an invoice for the customer. This keeps firms up to date on their inventory levels and assists them in keeping track of their sales.

Generating reports

QuickBooks Online enables businesses to produce reports on a variety of company metrics, including inventory levels, sales, and profitability. This enables firms to make educated judgments on the management of their inventory and to discover areas in which they can improve.

In a nutshell, the inventory management function of QuickBooks Online is an effective instrument that contributes to the efficient administration of inventory inside enterprises. Businesses are able to streamline their inventory management and make more informed decisions about their inventory if they measure the levels of their inventory, set up their inventory items, create buy orders, receive inventory, create sales orders, and fulfill orders. They can also generate reports to track these activities.

Payroll and Employees

The preparation of payroll and the management of employees are two crucial aspects of running a successful company. QuickBooks Online gives you access to a wide variety of tools and services that may assist business in managing payroll and other responsibilities linked to employees. We will discuss how you can use QuickBooks Online to handle your payroll and your employees in this part.

Setting Up Payroll in QuickBooks Online

Setting up your payroll system is the first thing you need to do in order to manage payroll with QuickBooks Online. In order to accomplish this goal, you will need to set up your payroll choices and enroll your workers to QuickBooks Online. After you have completed this step, you will be able to start the payroll processing for your employees.

You will need to carry out the following procedures in order to configure payroll in QuickBooks Online:

- Navigate to the Payroll Center

- Click on the "Employees" tab

- Click on "Add an employee"

- Enter the employee's information, including their name, address, and Social Security number

- Set up the employee's payroll preferences, including their pay rate, pay schedule, and tax withholding information

- Once you have added all of your employees, you can begin to process payroll

Processing Payroll

Once you have set up your payroll system, you can begin to process payroll for your employees. To do this, you will need to follow these steps:

- Navigate to the Payroll Center

- Click on the "Employees" tab

- Select the employees you want to pay

- Enter the hours worked for each employee

- Review the payroll summary to ensure accuracy
- Submit the payroll for processing

QuickBooks Online also allows you to set up direct deposit for your employees, which can save you time and money by eliminating the need to issue paper checks.

Managing Employee Information

QuickBooks Online gives you the ability to manage your employees' information in addition to letting you handle payroll processing. This involves keeping tabs on how many hours employees work, administering benefits, and scheduling vacation time for workers. In addition, you may utilize QuickBooks Online to produce employee reports, including payroll reports and reports on employees' time off.

Tracking Time

You have the option of manually entering employee hours, using a timer, or importing timesheets from a third-party program when you use QuickBooks Online to keep track of employee time. Other options include utilizing a timer. You are also able to keep track of paid time off and establish guidelines for overtime work.

Benefits Management

You are able to set up and manage employee perks, such as health insurance, retirement plans, and other benefits, with QuickBooks Online. Deductions for employee perks can also be set up, and the total cost of these benefits can be monitored.

Employee Self-Service

An employee self-service portal is also available through QuickBooks Online. Through this site, employees may examine their pay stubs, make changes to their personal information, and submit requests for time off. Both the administrative cost of addressing employee requests and the level of pleasure enjoyed by employees may decrease as a result of this.

Time Tracking

Despite the fact that keeping track of employees' clock-ins and clock-outs manually is a tedious task, managing a business successfully requires accurate timekeeping in order to be successful. QuickBooks Online simplifies and improves the efficiency of this process for its users by offering time tracking tools. These options provide users the ability to monitor staff hours, overtime, and even billable time for customers, making it feasible for them to manage all of these things. In the next section, we are going to look at the time tracking options that are available via QuickBooks Online.

It is necessary to have a strong grasp of how the time tracking component of QuickBooks Online is connected to the payroll tool in order to get things off the ground. It is required for you to have payroll switched on inside your QuickBooks Online account in order to take benefit of the time tracking feature that is available to you via that platform. Following the activation of payroll, you will be able to begin monitoring the amount of time spent on the job by each of your workers.

When you use the time tracking option in QuickBooks Online, one of the most major benefits of using this feature is that it eliminates the need to manually keep track of the amount of time that workers have put in. This is one of the most significant advantages of using this tool. Employees need to make use of the time tracking feature rather than being compelled to punch a time clock or fill out paper time sheets in order to keep track of the number of hours they have worked. This is because the time tracking function is more accurate. Workers are able to more simply and precisely report their time worked, which helps to reduce the possibility of mistakes happening and helps to guarantee that workers are paid accurately. Additionally, this helps to ensure that employees are paid appropriately.

When it comes to keeping track of their working hours, employees who are subscribed to QuickBooks Online have the choice of using either the web-based time tracking feature or the QuickBooks mobile app. Because it is web-based, the web-based time tracking application allows employees to log in to their own

QuickBooks Online accounts and manually enter the amount of hours that they have worked. They also have the opportunity to submit comments on the task that they have finished, which may be useful for monitoring the billable hours that they have worked. The mobile software makes it even easier for workers to keep track of the time they spend working by enabling them to easily enter the number of hours they have put in using their own mobile device, such as a smartphone or tablet. This makes it possible for employees to maintain an even more accurate record of the time they spend working. Because of this, the technique is far more effective.

Users are able to keep tabs on the billable time they spend on customers thanks to the time tracking function in QuickBooks Online, which is another benefit offered by this feature. This paves the way for a whole new set of opportunities and prospects. If you charge customers based on the amount of time spent on a project or assignment, then utilizing QuickBooks Online allows you to rapidly monitor the amount of time that was utilized on such projects and assignments. This comes in very handy if you change your customers by the hour. This might be helpful in ensuring that you are charging customers at an acceptable rate and that you are reimbursed for the amount of time that you spend working on clients' projects and that you are receiving payment for that time.

In addition to monitoring time worked by staff and time billed to customers, users of QuickBooks Online have the flexibility to specify their own preferences for how they wish to monitor time. This feature is in addition to the ability to measure time worked by staff. This involves evaluating the boundaries for overtime compensation as well as the suitable pay rates for workers based on the obligations of their jobs. Additionally, this includes calculating the appropriate pay rates for employees based on the responsibilities of their employment. This may help ensure that workers are paid properly for their work and that your company is in accordance with any relevant labor requirements that may apply to your company. This may also help ensure that employees are paid fairly for their work.

In summary, the time tracking function that is included in QuickBooks Online has the potential to be a very useful tool for businesses of any size. It is possible that it will simplify the process of documenting employee time, ensure that payroll is accurate, and help businesses in the process of getting paid for billable hours. Businesses who take use of this feature are able to increase the effectiveness of their operations, which in turn results in a decrease in the amount of time and money that is lost throughout the process.

Customization

QuickBooks Online gives customers access to a wide variety of customization options, which enables them to adjust the program to better suit the requirements of their own companies. These customization possibilities include the capability to create individualized fields, forms, reports, and responsibilities, as well as other individualized elements. In the following paragraphs, we will go through the available customization options in greater depth.

Custom Fields

Users of QuickBooks Online are given the ability to design and build their own fields, which may then be included on any of the software's forms, including invoices, sales receipts, purchase orders, and estimates. You may make use of QuickBooks Online's custom fields in order to record additional information that is not covered by the default fields that are offered by the software. An example of this would be a user creating a new field on an invoice to record the purchase order number of a particular customer. Individual forms or many forms can share the same set of custom fields after they have been established. When users create new forms, they may also put up templates for their own custom fields, which will save them time.

Custom Forms

In addition to this, users of QuickBooks Online have the ability to design their own forms, such as invoices, sales receipts, and estimates. Personalization options for design and branding can be incorporated into bespoke forms at the request of the user. Users have the ability to change the layout of their forms, including logos and photos, and select different font styles and color schemes. Users are able to make their own custom fields and include them in their forms if they choose to do so. In addition, users have the ability to create form templates, which will allow them to save time while building new forms.

Custom Reports

Users are able to monitor important financial parameters including as profit and loss, cash flow, accounts receivable and payable, and more with the help of the variety of basic reports that are included with QuickBooks Online. On the other hand, users could have certain reporting requirements that the standard reports are unable to satisfy. Users of QuickBooks Online have the ability to build personalized reports that may be adapted to meet their unique requirements. Users have the ability to select the data they would want to include in their reports, add filters to the data in order to enhance it, and personalize the report's structure and formatting.

Saved versions of customized reports may be accessed at a later time and exported to either Excel or PDF format.

Custom Roles

Users of QuickBooks Online are given the ability to establish custom roles, which provides them the ability to control access to various components of the software. Different categories of users, such as workers, contractors, and suppliers, can each have their own unique custom role that they can fill in the system. Users have the ability to configure permissions for viewing, creating, updating, and deleting transactions, as well as determine which tasks and features each role is authorized to access. Access to sensitive financial data, such as information on bank accounts and credit cards, can also be controlled through the use of custom roles.

Mobile App

In the fast-paced corporate climate of today, it is
essential to maintain connections with others and remain
on top of financials. QuickBooks Online is aware of this
requirement and satisfies it by offering a mobile app that
is compatible with both Android and iOS smartphones.
This section will walk you through the capabilities of the
QuickBooks Online mobile app and explain how it may
assist you in staying on top of the financials of your
company when you are away from your desk.

The QuickBooks Online mobile app is a powerful tool
that enables customers to remain connected to their
financials at all times and from any location. customers
may use the app using their mobile devices. The mobile
application provides a number of features that are aimed
at making the process of handling one's financial matters
while on the move easier to do. The following is a list of
some of the most important features included in the
QuickBooks Online mobile app:

- Dashboard: The dashboard of the mobile app provides an overview of your business financials. It displays a summary of your income, expenses, and profit and loss for the current period.

- Invoicing: With the mobile app, you can create and send invoices to customers on the go. You can also view the status of your invoices and get notified when they are paid.

- Expenses: The app allows you to track your business expenses by taking pictures of receipts and attaching them to transactions. You can also categorize expenses and add notes to transactions.

- Banking: You can connect your bank and credit card accounts to the app, and view transactions and balances in real-time. You can also add and match transactions, and even transfer funds between accounts.

- Time tracking: The mobile app allows you to track time for yourself or your employees. You can also add billable time to customer invoices.

- Reports: You can access a variety of reports on the mobile app, including profit and loss, balance sheet, and expense reports. You can also customize these reports to suit your needs.

- Contacts: The app allows you to manage your customers, vendors, and employees on the go. You can view contact information, add new contacts, and edit existing ones.

- Customization: The mobile app allows you to customize your invoices and estimates, as well as the look and feel of the app itself.

The QuickBooks Online mobile app, in general, makes it easier for consumers to keep track of their finances when they are away from their computers. It is an effective instrument that enables you to maintain a connection to your company at all times, regardless of where you may be. By managing your money using the app while you're on the move, you'll be able to cut down on wasted time and boost your productivity.

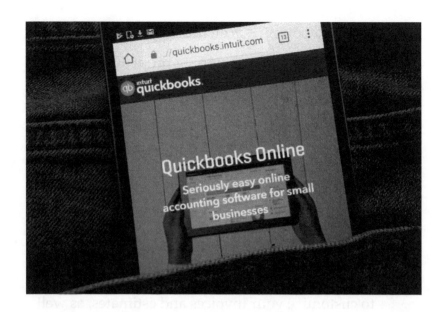

Piter2121/Depositphotos.com

Chapter 6

Glossary

Glossary of Accounting Terms

This "Glossary of Accounting Terms" section is an important component of any accounting reference, and that principle holds true for this guide to QuickBooks Online. Understanding accounting may be difficult due to the large number of specialized phrases and jargon that are used to express the many ideas and procedures involved in the field. When using QuickBooks Online, you may come across a number of different accounting terminology that are both common and significant; the purpose of this glossary is to give a clear and brief explanation of as many of those phrases as possible.

Because the terms are listed in alphabetical order, it is simple to traverse the page and locate the term you are searching for in a short amount of time. Each phrase is explained using language that is uncomplicated and straightforward, so giving a clear explanation of both its meaning and its context in the field of accounting. First, let's take a look at a few of the accounting terminology that may be included in this dictionary.

- Accounts payable: This refers to the money that a business owes to its suppliers or vendors for goods or services that have been purchased but not yet paid for.

- Accounts receivable: This term refers to the money that a business is owed by its customers or clients for goods or services that have been provided but not yet paid for.

- Accrual accounting: This is a method of accounting where transactions are recorded when they occur, rather than when payment is received or made. This method is used to provide a more accurate picture of a company's financial position.

- Asset: This refers to anything that a business owns that has value, such as cash, property, equipment, and inventory.

- Balance sheet: A balance sheet is a financial statement that provides a snapshot of a company's financial position at a specific point in time. It shows the company's assets, liabilities, and equity.

- Depreciation: This is the process of allocating the cost of an asset over its useful life. It's done to reflect the reduction in value of the asset over time.

- Equity: This refers to the value of a business after all liabilities have been deducted from its assets. It represents the ownership interest in the business.

- General ledger: This is the central repository of a company's accounting data. It contains all the transactions that have been recorded and is used to create financial statements.

- Income statement: An income statement is a financial statement that shows a company's revenue and expenses over a specific period of time. It's used to determine the company's profitability.

- Journal entry: This is the primary method of recording transactions in accounting. It's a record of a single transaction that shows the accounts affected, the amounts involved, and the date of the transaction.

- Liabilities: These are obligations that a business owes to others, such as loans, accounts payable, and accrued expenses.

- Profit and loss statement: This is another name for the income statement. It's used to show a company's revenue and expenses over a specific period of time.

- Reconciliation: This is the process of matching two sets of records to ensure that they are in agreement. For example, bank reconciliation involves comparing a company's bank statement with its general ledger to ensure that they match.

- Trial balance: This is a report that lists all the accounts in the general ledger along with their balances. It's used to ensure that debits and credits are equal.

This is only a tiny selection of the accounting terminology that are available in the glossary; there are many more. The glossary may help you navigate the complicated world of accounting and gain a better understanding of the financial health of your organization by giving definitions of key terms that are straightforward and to the point.

Glossary of QuickBooks Online Features

QuickBooks Online is robust accounting software that provides its users with a wide range of tools that may assist them in more efficiently managing their company's finances. A dictionary of some of the most essential features found in QuickBooks Online is provided below:

- Chart of Accounts: A list of all the accounts used in your business, such as assets, liabilities, revenue, and expenses. The chart of accounts is used to track the financial transactions of your business.
- Bank Feeds: A feature that connects your bank and credit card accounts to QuickBooks

Online, allowing you to import transactions and reconcile your accounts more quickly.

- Transactions: The financial transactions of your business, such as sales, expenses, and payments. QuickBooks Online allows you to create, edit, and manage transactions easily.

- Reports: A feature that allows you to generate a variety of financial reports, such as profit and loss statements, balance sheets, and cash flow statements. Reports can help you track your financial performance and make informed business decisions.

- Collaboration and User Management: A feature that allows multiple users to access and work on the same QuickBooks Online account. User management features let you control who has access to your data and what they can do with it.

- Advantages of QuickBooks Online: A section that discusses the benefits of using QuickBooks Online, such as accessibility from anywhere, automatic updates, and data security.

- Disadvantages of QuickBooks Online: A section that discusses the potential drawbacks of using QuickBooks Online, such as limited customization options and subscription fees.

- Comparison of QuickBooks Online and Desktop Software: A section that compares the features and functionality of QuickBooks Online with the desktop version of QuickBooks.

- Getting Started with QuickBooks Online: A section that provides a step-by-step guide to setting up your QuickBooks Online account and getting started with the software.

- Managing Sales and Income: A section that discusses how to manage your sales and income in QuickBooks Online, including creating invoices, tracking payments, and generating sales reports.

- Managing Expenses and Bills: A section that discusses how to manage your business expenses and bills in QuickBooks Online, including entering bills, paying bills, and generating expense reports.

- Managing Inventory: A section that discusses how to manage your inventory in QuickBooks Online, including creating and tracking products, recording inventory adjustments, and generating inventory reports.

- Payroll and Employees: A section that discusses how to manage payroll and employee data in QuickBooks Online, including setting up payroll, paying employees, and generating payroll reports.

- Time Tracking: A section that discusses how to track time and billable hours in QuickBooks Online, including setting up time tracking, creating timesheets, and generating time tracking reports.

- Customization: A section that discusses how to customize your QuickBooks Online account to meet your business needs, including customizing forms, adding custom fields, and creating custom reports.

- Mobile App: A section that discusses the QuickBooks Online mobile app, which allows you to manage your finances on the go, including creating and sending invoices, tracking expenses, and managing customers and vendors.

Tips for Using the Glossary

The glossary can be a useful tool for anyone using QuickBooks Online or working in the field of accounting. Here are some tips for effectively using the glossary:

- Use it as a reference guide: The glossary is a valuable reference guide to help you understand various accounting and QuickBooks Online terms. Instead of relying on guesswork or searching for explanations on the internet, consult the glossary for accurate definitions.

- Use it to learn new terms: The glossary can be a great resource for learning new accounting and QuickBooks Online terms. As you encounter unfamiliar terms, look them up in the glossary to learn their meanings and uses.

- Use it for training: If you are new to QuickBooks Online or need to train someone else, the glossary can be a helpful tool. Use it to explain various terms and concepts, and to help people understand how they relate to using the software.

- Use it for troubleshooting: If you encounter an error message or problem with QuickBooks Online, the glossary can be a helpful resource. Look up any unfamiliar terms or error messages in the glossary to understand what they mean and how to resolve the issue.

- Keep it updated: As QuickBooks Online and accounting terminology evolve, the glossary may need to be updated. Make sure to check for updates regularly and incorporate any new terms or definitions into your understanding.

- Don't rely on it too heavily: While the glossary can be a helpful tool, it's important to remember that it's not a substitute for a comprehensive understanding of accounting and QuickBooks Online. Use it as a reference and learning tool, but continue to deepen your knowledge and expertise through other resources and experiences.

By following these tips, you can effectively use the glossary to enhance your understanding of accounting and QuickBooks Online, and improve your overall productivity and efficiency.

Conclusion

QuickBooks Online is an excellent financial instrument that can be used by businesses of any size. It can keep track of money spent and received, manage merchandise, process payroll, and monitor labor hours, to name a few of its many helpful tasks. QuickBooks Online gives business owners simple access to the financial data of their companies around the clock thanks to the fact that it is located in the cloud. This book was written with the intention of providing new users of QuickBooks Online with all of the information that they need to get started with the software.

We covered a wide range of topics in this book, including how to set up an account, create a business profile, handle sales and expenditures, manage inventory, and log in to QuickBooks Online using the mobile app. This is just a sampling of the many topics covered. We have included both a lexicon of accounting terminology and a list of the most important features that can be found in QuickBooks Online in order to be of further assistance to the reader.

By centralizing and automating accounting operations, reducing the chance of human error, and giving access to trustworthy financial data on which to make decisions, QuickBooks Online enables businesses to save both time and money. This book was written with the intention of providing new users of QuickBooks Online with all of the information that they need to get started with the software.

QuickBooks Online is a tool that is essential to have at your disposal as a proprietor of a company if you want to improve the efficiency of your accounting processes and get a more in-depth understanding of your company's financial information. It should come as no surprise that one of the accounting software programs with the highest number of users is QuickBooks Online due to the abundance of helpful features and user-friendly interface that it offers.

And now, first of all, thank you for purchasing this book **QuickBooks Online For Beginners.** I know you could have picked any number of books to read, but you picked this book and for that I am extremely grateful.

If you enjoyed this book and found some benefit in reading this, I'd like to hear from you and hope that you could take some time to post a review on Amazon.

I want you, the reader, to know that your review is very important.
I wish you all the best in your future success!

Made in United States
Troutdale, OR
07/25/2023

11538518R00076